T0063024

PEACH COUNTRY

PEACH COUNTRY

POEMS BY

NONDWE MPUMA

UHLANGA

2022

Peach Country

© Nondwe Mpuma, 2022, all rights reserved

First published in Durban, South Africa by uHlanga in 2022

UHLANGAPRESS.CO.ZA

Distributed outside southern Africa by the African Books Collective

AFRICANBOOKSCOLLECTIVE.COM

ISBN: 978-0-620-98688-5

Editing, cover design and typesetting by Nick Mulgrew

Proofread by Karina Szczurek

Cover image by Shakil Solanki | @SHAKILSOLANKI_STUDIO

The body text of this book is set in Garamond Premier Pro 11PT on 15PT

❀

Some of the poems in this collection have been previously published, sometimes in different forms: "Childhood" and "Home" in the *McGregor Poetry Festival Anthology 2017*, and *Cutting Carrots the Wrong Way* (uHlanga, 2017); "Morning is the time we count the dead" in *New Coin*; and "The first day of mourning," "List of things that are bad luck" and "Taking into account" in *Stanzas*. In addition, "Childhood" has been previously broadcast on Kaya FM.

ACKNOWLEDGEMENTS

The original version of this collection was submitted as part of my Master's in Creative Writing at the University of the Western Cape. My sincerest gratitude to Kobus Moolman for the belief, supervision, guidance and support.

To my mother, ndiyabulela maRhadu.

To my family, thank you for being repositories and my deepest well of support.

To my friends and peers, thank you for the encouragement.

To all the publications – including *WritingThreeSixty*, *Underground: Art and Literary Journal*, *New Contrast*, *New Coin*, *Stanzas*, *Five Points* and *Taking Liberties* – editors, festival organisers and poetry spaces – including the McGregor Poetry Festival, the Commons, The Red Wheelbarrow, Open Book Festival, Franschhoek Literary Festival, and US Woordfees – that have given my work room, thank you.

A special thanks to Nick and uHlanga, for carrying my words.

– N.M.

CONTENTS

3

For Sinalo Mpuma and Thandolwethu Bidla

1

Eden

We begin with plein and pleasure,
let it be known.

There are no hills and mountains.
We won't find bones here, not Adam's,
not Eve's.

Beloved, we are too close to waters.
Our totems fear the seas.

Between us
lust sits in burgundy.
We are easily movable in the work of the Lord.

Initiations

The christening waters
make the journey from her forehead to her hair.

She jumps over a fire in a beaded shirt,
warming her hymen.

She emerges from the river
with snakes hanging off her neck.

Her knees become a starless sky and her feet are a map of the other world.
She knows that an animal must be skinned to get to the bone.

She emerges from the river
with whites clinging to her bosom in the heat of praise.

She rips through the meat
of her brother's circumcision.

She spears the cow through the heart,
concluding her births.

Childhood

it was not too long ago that coming home during *The Bold and the Beautiful* caught us a hiding we never returned home on time when fetching water the bursts of water-filled condoms tied our legs to the tap our return from herding the goats led us to the big tree on the hill where we picked and plaited grass skipping ropes and we jumped to the months of the year *ooNozizwe ooShigoshi* and our heads spun from rounds of *ooSamthumela* sometimes the skipping rope was replaced by my grandmother's old ripped pantyhose where our young throats never tired from singing *uXoshiwe* other times the skipping ropes and the pantyhose were replaced by a plastic ball an old enamel dish and tin cans and after hours at play with shaking hands behind our backs we tried to sneak into the kitchen where we had left mountains of breakfast dishes but they would have disappeared and our grandmother would be waiting for us to throw out the dirty water with her face twisted up in unspoken anger we told tales about the goats running away from us that saved us from our grandmother's shouts most times we were not that lucky and often bribed her by spring-cleaning the home

Pastoral

Cows stop the cars.

They cross over to the marsh like soldiers on parade.

Their hips are those of belly dancers.

Pockets of dark clouds promise rain.

Wild lavender waves in the wind.

A bird is splayed on the pavement.

Two dirty zebra-striped cats scavenge in the bins lining the wall.

A heron languidly herds.

The cows are Moses. They part the grass and lavender to reach the river.

They drink from a river of diapers.

There is a goat for every occasion

There was one for my birth. Where my father's hand held mine
and touched it to the goat's forehead and my grandmother spoke her
hopes and my light into the goat's death. There was another when
I passed grade three. The goat was a gift, not to be killed. It was a
buck and fathered many children, but none of them could be his,
because all kids belong to nannies in the goat-verse. When my
bleeding started, I wore a goat on my wrist for the first time.
Its gall bladder was taken out as an offering to the shades. One tear
was dropped onto my hand to lick and the rest moisturised my skin.
It's no wonder I glow.

Chewing bubble-gum at the virginity testing ceremony

An older woman came up on the stage.
She had no speech written out, but the outer corners of her eyes were slanted by wisdom.
Her speech began, "Ndizothetha ngenyama yezifebe."
Chewing gum will force your legs open and pull a baby out of you.
The tension between the upper and lower molars will pull more babies out.
Suddenly you will be a female dog whose mouth has been pinned open for all dogs.
Once your teeth clamp down on it you are destroyed for life.

From God's stool in summer
– after Anne Carson

Ocean dune
Time eats you when the rain and winds come
Open boat
You are my ark when we rise and approach the shore
Your hands
Met mine in the middle of giving grace
Stories
That lie before us in trinkets of light
Clouds and tears
Are thieves that steal the sun
Dog
He howls at us

IBhayibhile yesiXhosa

A monolithic God waits for praises on a mountain.
This time a lost bible is its own creation:
uQamata shipped as the God of Egypt
and the son of Mary.

uQamata has always been a god of loss –
lost teachings
and prayers
and subjects.

This god of lonesomeness sits in wait for a mention in passing.

The festive season

It is December.

And the uncle from eGoli has arrived. His new used car stands
    in front of the veranda. We anticipate our own joy-rides
    down the road. He blesses us with five- and two-rand coins.
    The smell of the KFC he has brought carries through the
    two-bedroom house. We stare at his bag predicting that
    sweets will fall out. We imagine how we will wake the next
    morning with lollipop dummies hanging out of our mouths,
    staining our pillows.

He has arrived with evidence of his gold digging.

Tornadoes

One late spring, in the morning of summer,
a woman sees the tail of inkanyamba.

An orchestra of tins, pots, pans and drums
play in the air,

small prayers that the unpainted roofs
are not mistaken for iziziba.

In the tail end of summer,
we watch peacocks flare their feathers to their beloveds.

History of the year

EyoMqungu [tambuki grass]
The god of beginnings

We are a people of thatch
A weaving people
Of thorned invasive roots
A people of cattle wealth

EyoMdumba [swelling grain]
A baptism

All things living require birth
And birth comes after swelling
We are a people of swelling seeds
And grain

EyoKwindla [first fruits]
The god of war

We hail from peach country
In buckets and enamel bowls on the side of the road
Rotting peaches, worm-invaded peaches
In tight-lidded used mayonnaise bottles waiting for Christmas peaches
We are a people at war against dry lips and grumbling tummies

uTshaz' iimpuzi [withering pumpkins]
Opening flowers

As living things are born, they contend with death
Death, like age is not kind
Death reminds us of hunger / the preparation for
    the wind-blades of winter

EyeCanzibe [the winter star]
The goddess of fertility

We are of the stars, the brightest in the universe
We are of the Old Man of the South Pole, the Golden Earth
Navigators to the Nile
We know weathering seasons from the sky

EyeSilimela [Pleiades]
The goddess of marriage

God favours three and seven
The trinity and perfection
We read the endings and beginnings in the stars
We know that the plough is nigh

2

Loved-one follow (Eden II)

Enter, in the beginning of winter
with weeds and thorns sprouting between amagade.
The peach trees are dry at this time of the year.
They stand like scarecrows in the middle of
harvest time.

Walk slowly in the peppering salt-granules of frost.
Feel the toes inside soft leather curdle like burnt custard.
Watch your hands turn purple because when the sun shines on snow,
the cold engulfs the valley.
Watch your hands turn purple like fading black hair dye.

Don't rush for spring and summer,
this is not the garden of Eden, forever flowered and green.
It is too brown to be Eden, too affected by the temperament of clouds
    and sun and sky.
Don't rush for spring and summer, even
though our mothers' tongues tell us that these are times of plenty.

Watch as peach-pink blossoms sprout before the leaves and fruit.
Enter, in spring, where life is held in blossoms as it is in moles on skin.
Till and weed.
Clear out all the thorns.
Uncover the rich red-brown-black soil.

Seeds can be sown here,
where coils uncoil and straighten in the rays of the sun
and grass strands begin to bear seeds
that we can twist to rope to game.

In summer, a time of plenty,
I spread leaves like puzzle pieces.
I want to create an Eden forever green.
Recreate that moment between man and serpent.
The breeze is disobedient, and the leaves fleet away like dust.

Dream

I am in a burning hut with snakes
and you know how to watch quietly
and we both leave with minds intact.

I'm drowning in a shallow river
my arms flail around, so you know how to wait
and I love you for waiting.

In this dream I'm covered by a swarm of bees like a second layer of skin.
They begin to weave honey from my pores.
You don't start a fire, you don't gather smoke, and here I know you
    love me.

The first day of mourning

A crow perches itself on the corner of the rooftop.

The society ladies sway into the yard with boxes of long-life milk on their heads and Shoprite bags swinging from their wrists.

In the kitchen, pots of Glen tea are boiling away.

In the mattress room a lone figure covered in black sits with her head lowered.

The society ladies enter telling her that they are there to hold her, to shed tears and to strengthen her.

They say:

that God gives and He takes,

that He is there to hold her hand like a baby learning to take her first steps,

that she should be happy that her husband is at rest in the land of milk and honey,

that his bones will join the old ones and she can always call upon them to protect her,

that he is at home below.

She, with eyes cast down to the blanket folded across her legs, thinks of how the sun sucks the life out of a fallen leaf.

Human experience

A man has such great expectations of a baby boy
that he drops him on his head in an examination of strength,
preaching that he who survives is fit for a world where death can,
with a flick of a finger, stop a man mid-step.

A woman cradles a baby girl's virginity like annealed glass.
Maidenhood is measured by the hymen.

A child becomes a boy becomes a man.
A child becomes a girl becomes a woman.
The child dies for the boy, the boy dies for the man, the man dies.
The child dies for the girl, the girl dies for the woman, the woman dies.

Taking into account

the crooked left toe
that crashed against the corner of the coffee table
357 moles on the parts of her body that she could see
she was going to live for a very long time
her breasts gradually wanting to feel the earth
she hasn't even had them fill with milk
the receding hairline
she knows that control has a price
the c-shaped scar on her hand
someday it will be a marker to identify her

faded lines from her waist to just above her knees
they mark the fluctuations of fashion
the potholes on her thighs
painting a picture of all the meals that have nourished her
an underfoot scar
where she was cut by a cracked tile in a public pool
her widening loony-toon-rabbit-like gap
genetic inheritances seem permanent
her armpit opens showing discolouration and a faint line
that is a reminder of the ingrown boil surgery that she had at the age of 16

what else could she have left behind?

Morning is the time we count the dead
– after Takako Arai

First, the ones who come out of the womb silent.
Second, the ones who die before the fall of their deciduous teeth.
Third, the ones who have fought and lost against old age.
Fourth, the ones who mourn the dying.
Fifth, the ones who live dying.
Sixth, the ones devoured by abnormal growths.
Seventh, the ones who fly themselves out of windows.
Eighth, the ones who mourn the ones who should be dead.
Finally, the ones who mourn each morning.

Home

and we fetched them from the airport
and home arrived with nightly prayers and steam pudding
and in the evenings my mother cooked pap
and vleis and we sat around the stumpy glass table
and watched *Animal Farm* on SABC News
and we threw stones at Napoleon
and I passed my grandfather *Eight Days in September*
and with old eyes he read until he had to walk out for a smoke
and night came

and he called utamncane and checked on the cows
and he checked on the sheep and the chickens and his wild horse
and the church list
and the goat that had disappeared for three days
and when the beds began to call, my grandmother began
    uKristu Mkhululi Wethu
and our uneven voices were capable of breaking windows
and we knelt in thanks to the Almighty
and after the Lord's prayer was sung, grandmother taught my cousin
    the words to *Nkosi Ndithembe Wena*

and after Amen we answered the beds' prayers.

Identifying witches

The old lady who is the last of her generation walks past.
The pleats on her face fold all the way down to her neck.
She totters as though every step needs a pause before the next.
She lives in a rondavel.
She is a witch.

The little girl whose clothes carry the smell of smoke
with her legs folded and held captive by her stick-like arms sits alone.
Last night's empty dinner plate is drawn in ash on her lips and
drawn with ribs on her belly.
She is a witch.

The man who was dropped on his head by his father
speaks to himself from sunrise to sunset.
He picks up pieces of trash and is always, always alone.
He walks barefoot with his sixth toe on show and his hands are dry
    and creased.
He, too, is a witch.

List of things that are bad luck

Watching donkeys give birth.
There are things that must never be seen
lest we lose our sight.

Weeping at night.
One can never be too careful with the approach of the witching hour
and no woman readily volunteers to be a spinster.

Eating with the left hand.
There is something disturbing about having similarities with monkeys
and not being right.

Being behind someone or
giving something to someone behind their back or behind someone else's back.
Backs carry many burdens and most frightening is the burden of bad luck.

Closing all the doors and windows during a storm.
Lightning requires an entrance
and an exit.

Refusing ceremonial meat.
The ancestors hold
generational grudges.

Mumbling angrily about a parent.
They are closer to where feet turn and toes point to the sky
and once at this place they become those who hold grudges.

Waiting

We look for the sun.
The clouds hang like burnt buns
without butter. There will be no rain.
Let us not let the grey cause us pain.

The flowers are open
and bees drain pollen.
The horses run across the mountains.
We must look at all these lives without stains.

Untitled

Here sunflowers are picked from the side of the road
and hid from the sun.
Here water is encased in the veins of leaves.

Here rain is a memory.
Here the horse neighs like a dog.
Here hunger howls in the wind like a whisper.

Here doors and bars are locked, and the key lost.
Here is a snarky road.
Here are mumbled prayers from a single soul.

Here is a face moulded by sixteen-hours-working.
Here is a girl who becomes a woman who becomes old. She becomes.
Here is a winning lottery ticket for a million tears.

3

Eden III

Let us borrow love.
uQamata only listens from the mountain.

Let us pour sunflower petals dunked in perfume
down each other's necks. Oshun will approve.

Invisible red strings tie us together like infinite leashes.
We know too well that a broken string never regains perfection.

Allow us Cupid's arrows.
We will pierce each other.

Let us only have life like the bristlecone pine.
We have no need for knowledge, for good or evil.

Borrow us time as a companion.

Three ceremonies

1

With God's blessing the happy couple walk down the aisle. Comforted by their *Dominion over the fish of the sea and over the fowl of the air, and over the cattle, and over all the earth*. Comforted by the capacity of her womb to hold and not by the years that she will remain barren and all the years that he will sow his seed in other pastures over the earth. In her champagne gown and him, in his charcoal tuxedo, the happy couple walk down the aisle in a church as one flesh blessed by the trinity.

2

She is dressed by her mother and sister in an indigo Three Cats dress that complements her husband's shirt. She sits on a mat, her head lowered, counting ants. Before they throw blankets over her and her new family puts her in a thick off-white cotton gown with black trimming on the skirt and shawl. The old woman in the middle of the tent, next to her new granddaughter-in-law, holds a full jug of brew, she pours three drops on the ground while calling out three of the nearest clan names and asks them to open. In quick succession the young woman is changed and more blankets are thrown over her, and he sits and marvels over what a blushing bride she is, she who will brew beer, brew children, brew a home all for him.

3

He enters her father's kraal with a gift that will make mouths move, and a bottle of Klipdrift Export under his armpit. He gifts her father with a cow and takes his leave. There is no special dress for the day, she is in everyday clothes, in the home that she will leave for her own. Her family throws more blankets over her. They will keep her warm when he leaves.

At the end

Burning rocks war in the sky
mapping
where you
     and
         I
             end.
         Even

   the
       road
           shifts

       and
  meanders
       around

           trunks
       and
  rivers
       for
         us.

In this moment we abandon fibre optics and satellites.
Our mouths do what they do best.
Words dissipate with time; we have made them expensive.
Like air they become thin, only to reverberate throughout the cosmos.

A courting

I want to leave you thinking about what the cat thinks as he chases the mouse, or feeds on a pigeon under the table.

I want you to wonder about the pregnant cloud that refuses to give birth.

I want you to look at the sheep that is jealous about its breasts even as its lamb wastes away and be in awe.

I want to lead you to the holes in the fence that the chickens keep breaching.

I want you to fear the cows because they have horns that we should probably fear and they have grudges that they should probably avenge.

At night-time I want you to see the fullness of the moon and the dust of matter in the sky.

Grace

Burnt offering

The enamel plate is the altar,
a daughter of Levi burns and blows imphepho to the dead.
She goes through the holy spirits to the son.

Gain offering

The mealies are ground to powder,
the toil a message tied to the Songlines.
The powder turns to sorghum beer, a drink for the dead,
    a Holy Communion.

Peace offering

Here is a slaughter
of welcome and thank-you.
The headless chicken chasing its murders.

Sin offering

The white buck, having fathered no kids, is offered.
Its bile is smeared on our faces and seasons the towel-lining of
    its stomach and raw liver.
The white skin tucked between base and mattress vacuums the
    impure crumbs left behind.

Guilt offering

The enamel plate my altar, three candles in three colours burning,
imphepho burning, snuff burning, goat bones burning.
I leave my buttons without twine.

The diagnosis

I understand that your belly cracks beneath the weight of the air that the blood pushes to your tail bone and that your eyes every now and then see dark spots and you suspect that you have dizzy spells and you think that sitting feels like you have borrowed your grandmother's eighty-year-old body and kneeling brings no relief other than allowing the air to settle heavily on your tail and ovaries and I remember from our last meeting that when the headaches come your head becomes a forgotten boiling egg and that you think the murmurs in your hands indicate that you have a mild case of vertigo and that lying down eases the air in your waist and you get an urge to pig out on junk food and your mouth is as dry as a burnt piece of steak and you guzzle water down like an endless river and if I am to understand you correctly all these symptoms occur at that time of the month?

Cramming

She starts with the small tears in her skin.
Counts their doubling, their acupunctural placements,
their guarding of evil.

She counts the number of times that the car bounces over pebbles.
She saves how each house is positioned, even the one that she grew knowing as ruins
where fruit waited for the eager picker. How even nature since abandoned that oasis.

She looks at the shape of the hill.
It holds the marks of water-fetching trips.
In some place, some where, she logs faces and names like a coroner's report.

With the breeze harsh,
she wonders if it will stop feeling like losing a limb.

Definition

The paved road,
a path to a Wendy house accustomed to the beating of a pipe.
A chair,
a stump of an old tree in a kitchen.
A Jewel,
a stove that will outlive us all.

The beach,
a holiday I could never reach.
Sand,
carried with beach-dog oil to keep the ancestors at bay.
A gravel road,
the intimacy of a plank in the back of a van.

Smoke,
my grandfather's red Peter Stuyvesant.
Refinery,
I could smoke you like you smoke me and together we would
    incinerate the world.
A stop sign.
Does the meteorite shower dissipate in your presence?

A sleepless night

Arms are wilted spinach.
At this time of night, the head is heavy with sleep.
Suck the sleep with a syringe;
draw it the way laxatives do a full stomach.

Legs are peeled tree stalks.
The spine moves the bones to the left, then to the right
and finally turns the bones to look up at the shadows on the ceiling.
A spider is at home near the light bulb.

Night does not flood the room with darkness.
In the left corner near the bookshelf, another spider weaves a cocoon
    around a dead moth.
The eyes look because the spine has turned the bones left again.
The head will be heavy for another week.

The sea said, "Come closer"

But I will not throw myself into you. I will stand here far from your sand and shells. I will sit with you under the fading moon and listen to you rumble. I will not come any closer to your leopard leaps. I will not be your prey.

I wait for morning to pour some of you into the Coke bottle beside me. I wait for the afternoon to sprinkle you around my yard. I wait for evening to come back to this moment, to listen to you give and take, and give once more.

To all the deities I know

For those who know my name through smoke between our worlds,
        I ask you to open.
To you who knew my name but for the foaming at your mouths,
        you live with me.
To you who like a dog in shared custody wanted me –
        I want you like everyday's most pressing need.
I know that you open to those who left too young.
        You are my time's regret.

uHlanga

POETRY FOR THE PEOPLE

— RECENT RELEASES IN ISIXHOSA —

Ilifa ngu Athambile Masola

Unam Wena ngu Mthunzikazi A. Mbungwana

— RECENT RELEASES IN ENGLISH —

Jesus Thesis and Other Critical Fabulations by Kopano Maroga

An Illuminated Darkness by Jacques Coetzee

Still Further: New Poems, 2000–2020 by C.J. Driver

— RECENT AWARD-WINNING TITLES —

Everything is a Deathly Flower by Maneo Mohale
WINNER OF THE 2020 GLENNA LUSCHEI PRIZE FOR AFRICAN POETRY
FINALIST FOR THE 2020 INGRID JONKER PRIZE

All the Places by Musawenkosi Khanyile
WINNER OF THE 2020 SOUTH AFRICAN LITERARY AWARD FOR POETRY
FINALIST FOR THE 2020 INGRID JONKER PRIZE

Zikr by Saaleha Idrees Bamjee
WINNER OF THE 2020 INGRID JONKER PRIZE

AVAILABLE FROM GOOD BOOKSTORES IN SOUTH AFRICA *&* NAMIBIA
& FROM THE AFRICAN BOOKS COLLECTIVE ELSEWHERE

UHLANGAPRESS.CO.ZA

Printed in the United States
by Baker & Taylor Publisher Services